At the Hair Salon

Over and Over Ag

I0805274

Seth Matthas

COMPUTER SCIENCE For the REAL World™

Rosen Classroom™

Today, I'm going to the hair salon. That's where I have my cornrows done. Cornrows are tiny braids.

Cornrows take a long time. My mom and I go to the hair salon for the whole day! She will get braids too.

I love to try new hairstyles. Sometimes I keep my hair plain. Sometimes I have beads in my hair. I like cornrows best.

Miss Layla is my hairdresser. First, she uses a comb to part my hair. She parts my hair down the middle.

Miss Layla takes a rubber band. She ties the rest of my hair so it is out of the way.

Next, Miss Layla starts a braid. She divides one of the rows into three parts.

Miss Layla braids the three sections one over the other. She starts at the front of my head. She braids down to my neck.

Miss Layla takes a tiny rubber band. She puts the rubber band around my braid to hold it in place.

Miss Layla has to do the steps over and over again. She makes many braids on my head.

My cornrows are done. Cornrows are important in my family's history. I am proud to wear them!

Words to Know

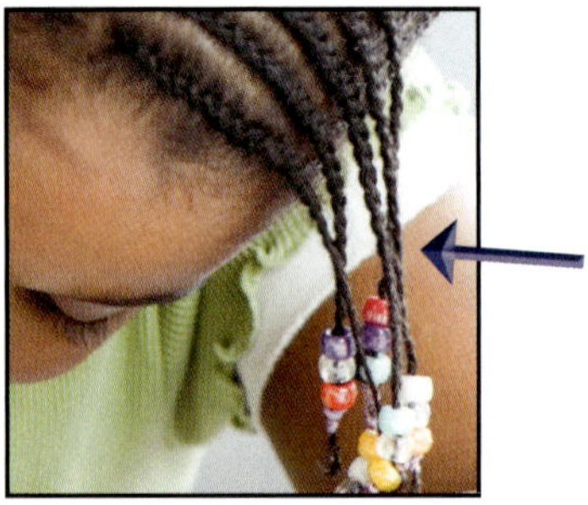

braid

cornrow

hairdresser

hair salon

rubber band